Vol 13

MAZE

FOR KIDS

Ages 4-6

MAZE BOOK

f /MySweetBooks1

/MySweetBooks1

/MySweetBooks1

/MySweetBooks

Email Us : mysweetbooks1@gmail.com

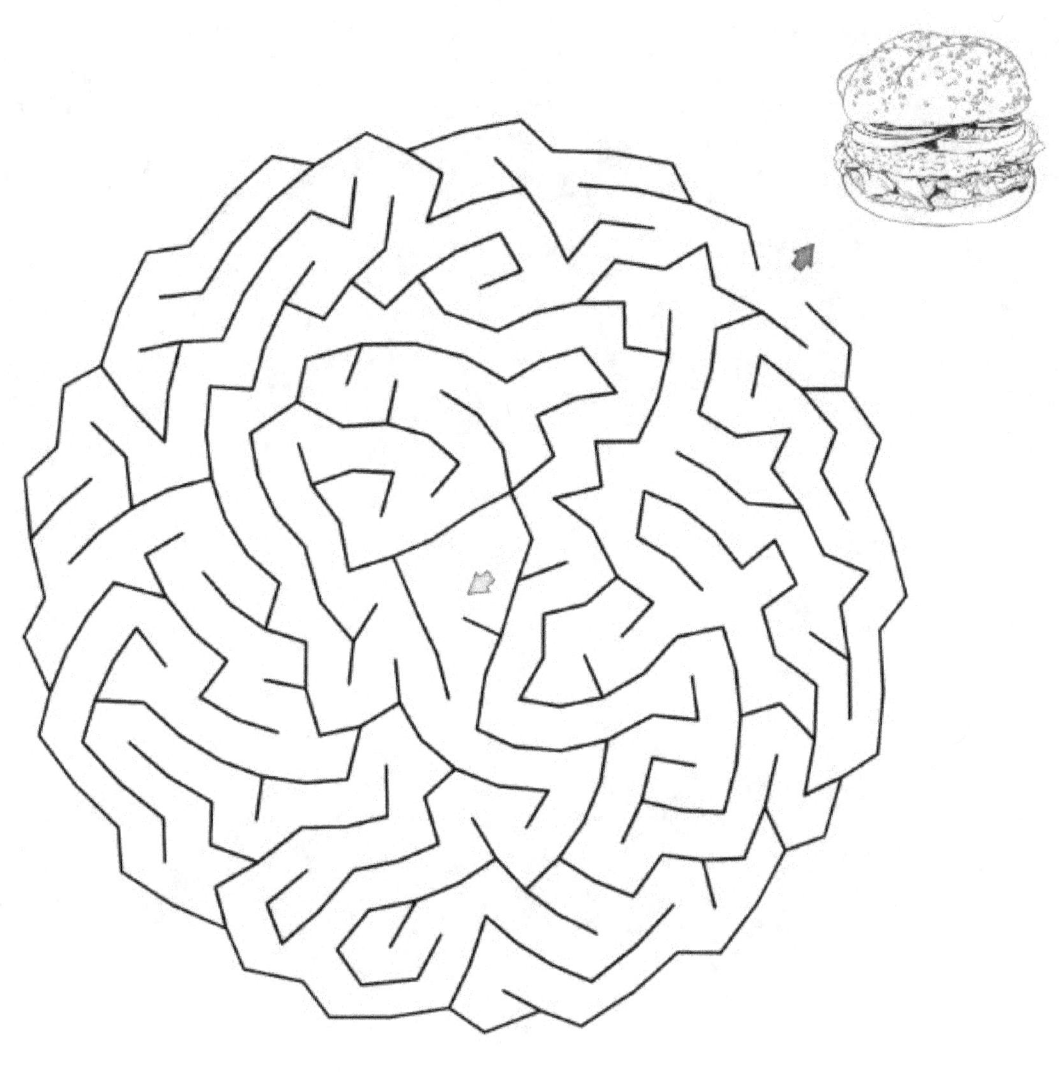

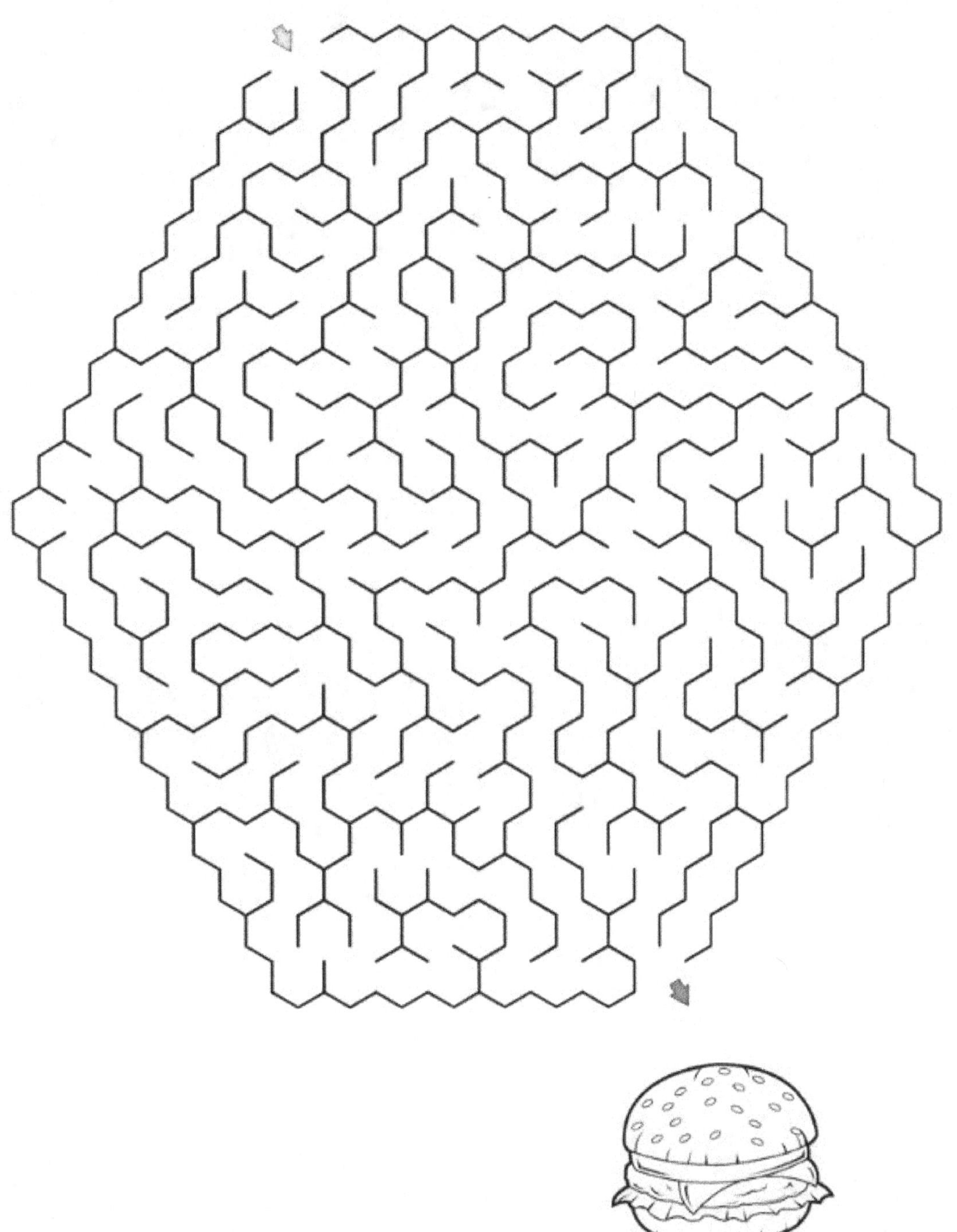

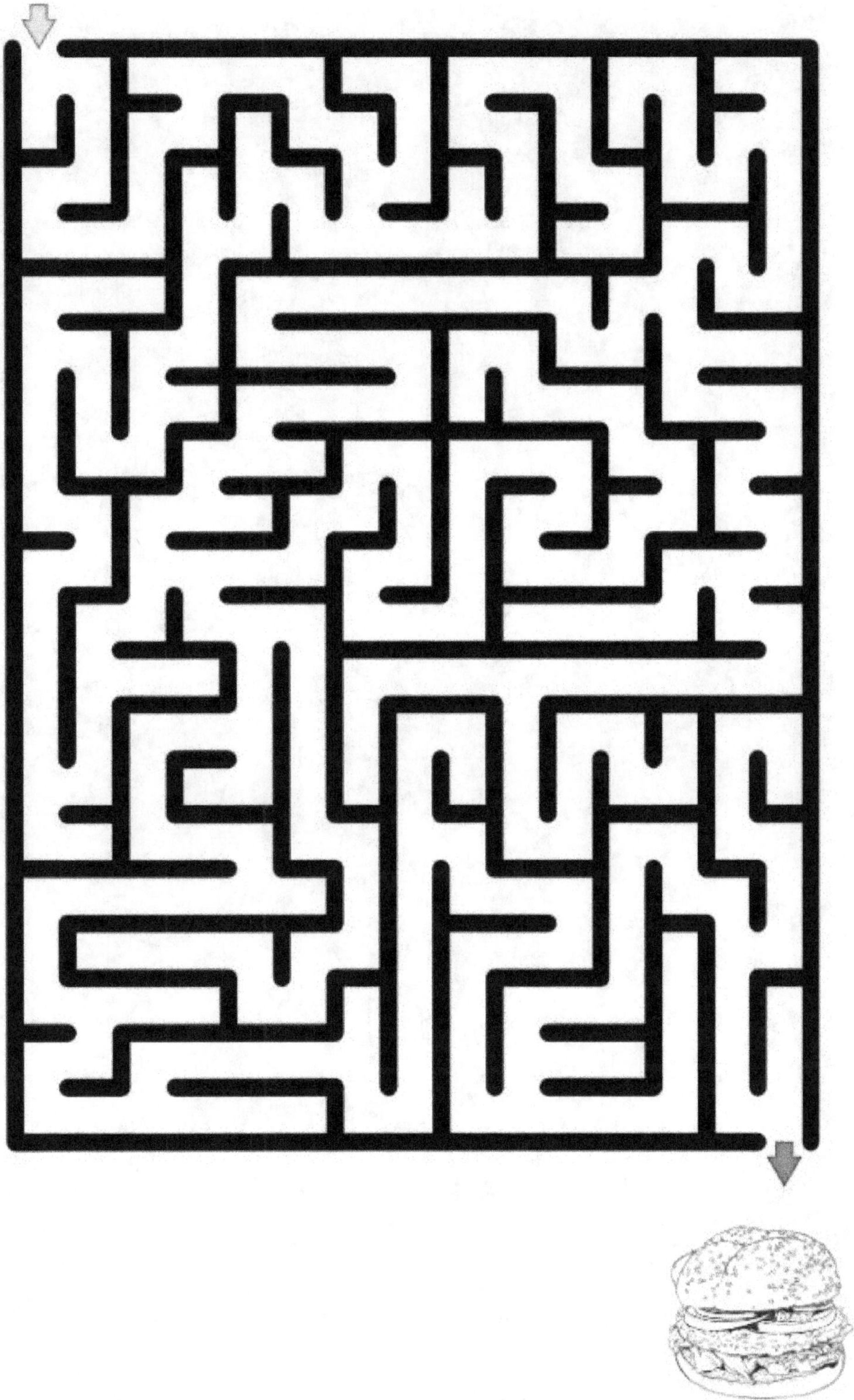

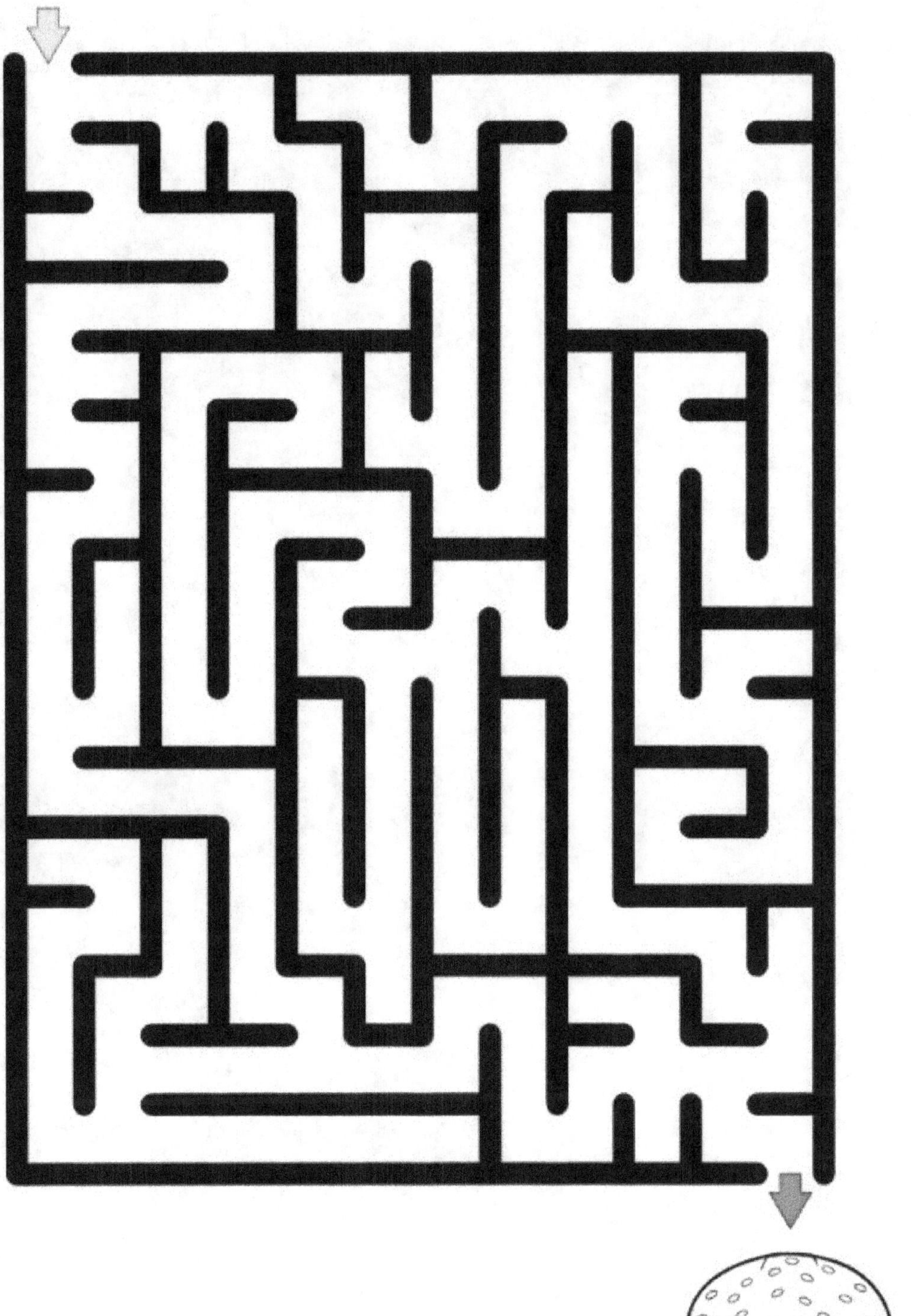

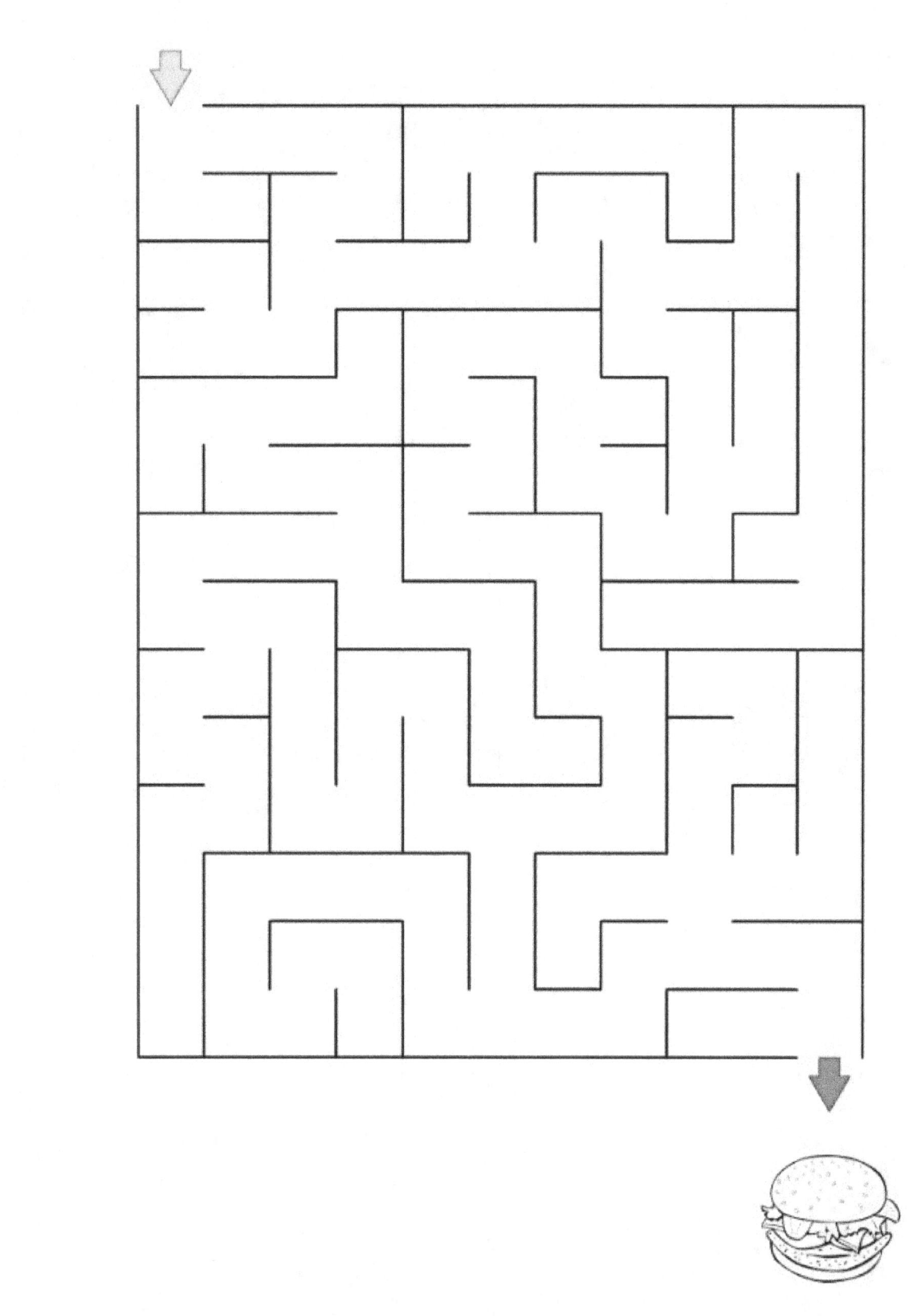

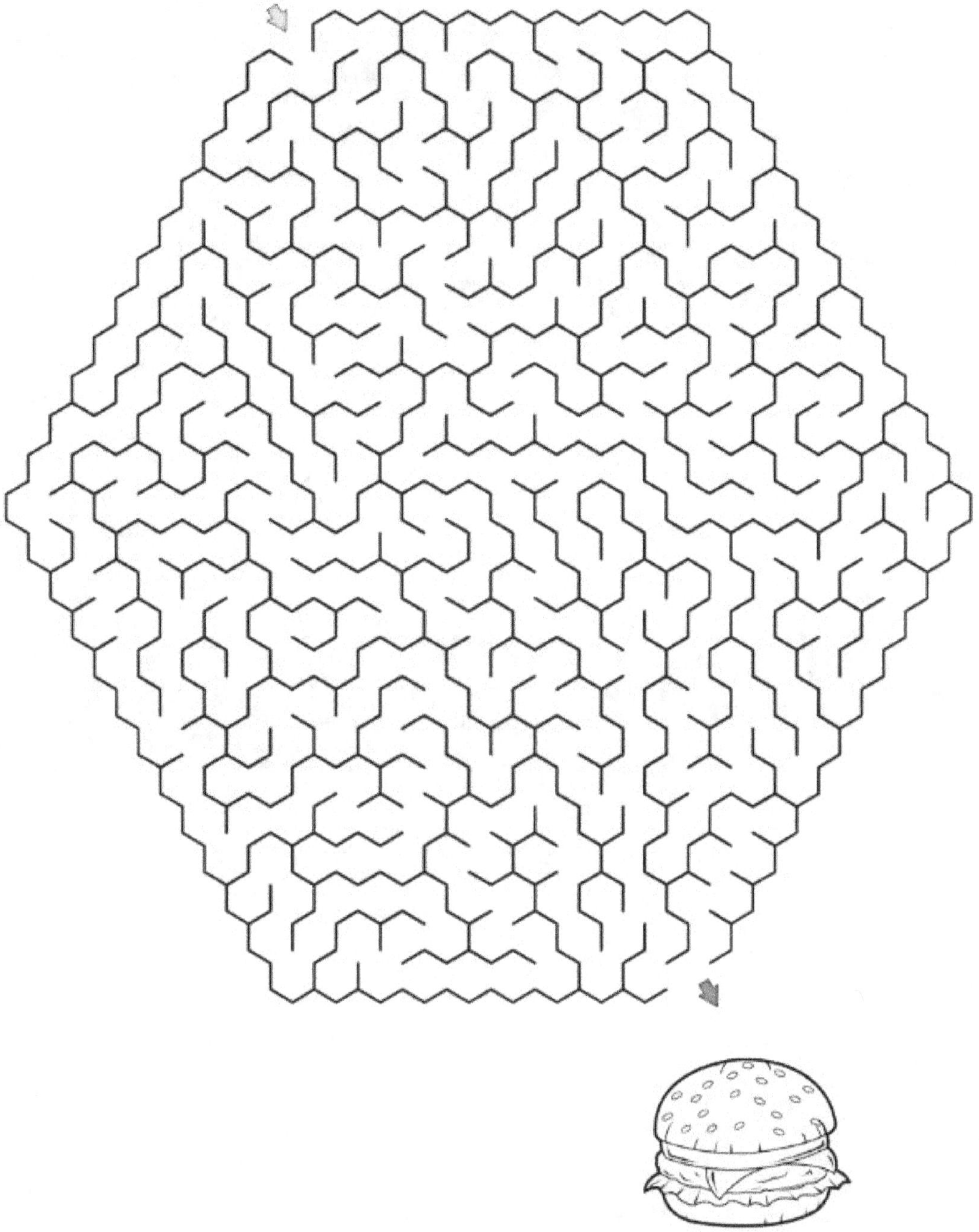

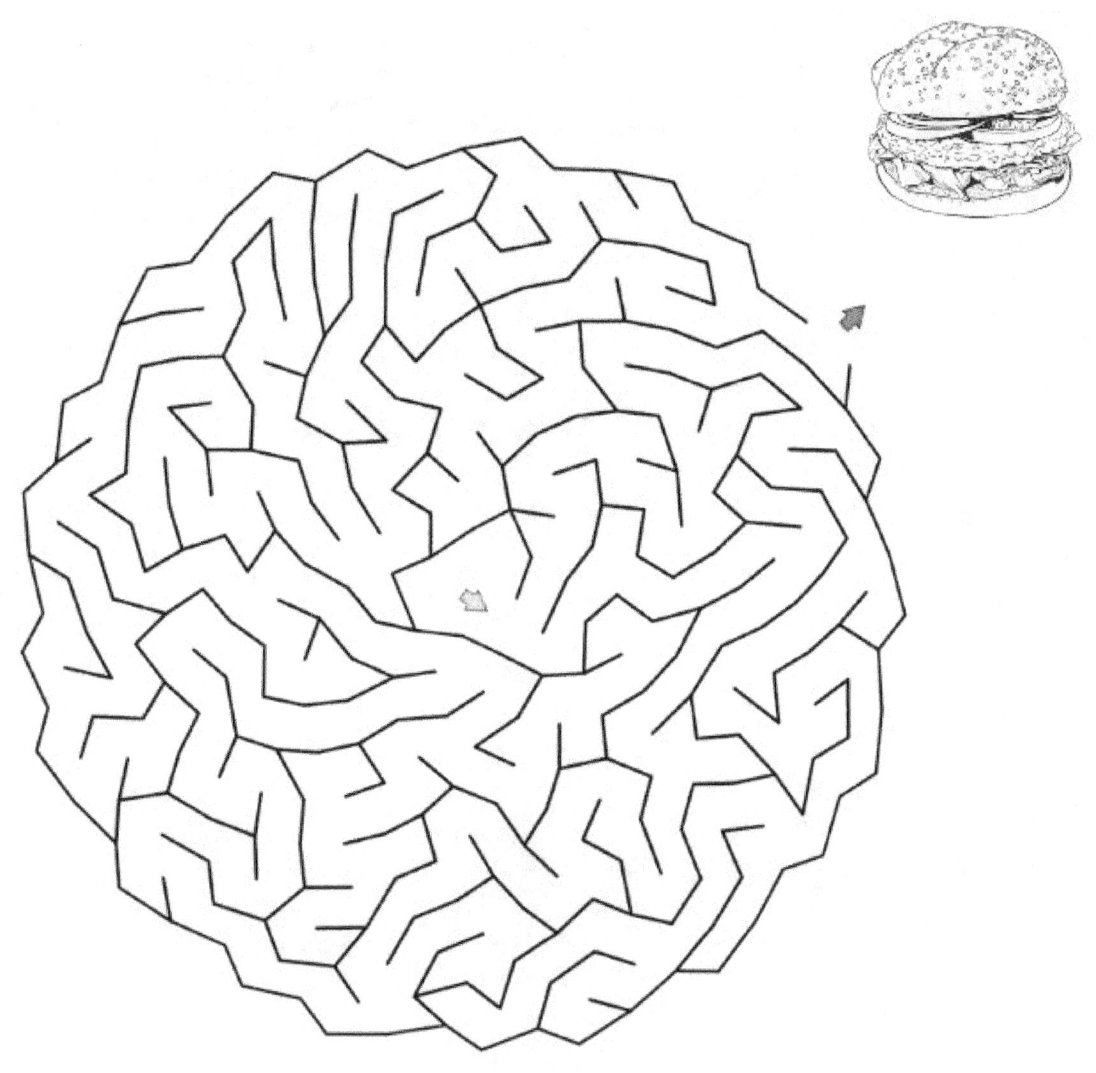

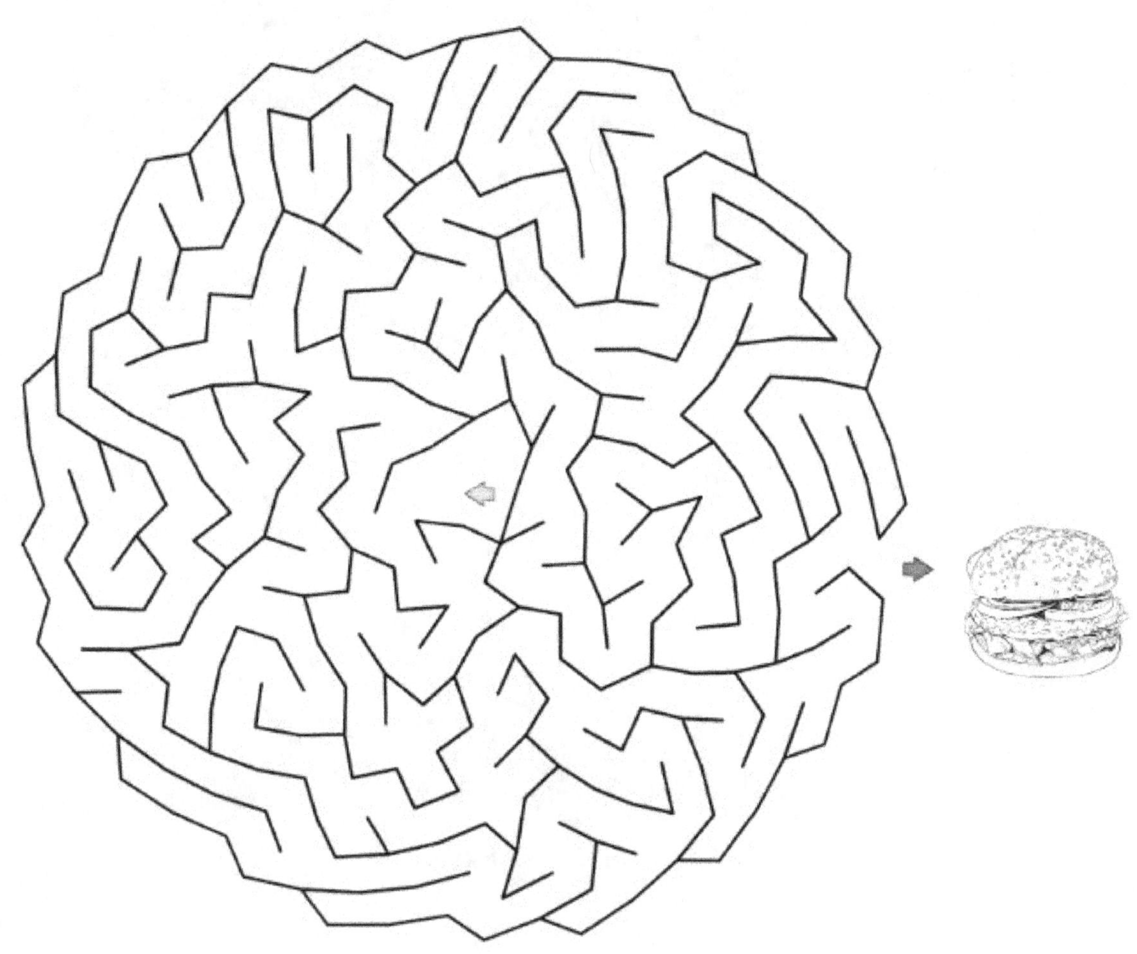

www.ingramcontent.com/pod-product-compliance
Lightning Source LLC
Chambersburg PA
CBHW081737250726
48657CB00010B/3309